Delay of Game

A woman's unconditioned intuition

C E D R I C K   W I L S O N

ISBN: 1463513933
ISBN-13: 9781463513931

The GMC
(Grown Man Club)

The GMC is a social group of MEN who strive to uphold the title of a man. No matter your race, religion, or age, all men have similar character traits. One that is MANDATORY of any GMC member is respect for women. The GMC will do whatever lies within its power to contribute to the growth and resurrection of respectable and honorable men in today's society. Better fathers, husbands, and overall households are the ongoing goals. I encourage every man to take heed to the definition of the word GENTLEMEN. Somehow, it has become a word thought to be a sign of weakness and not respected amongst men.

1) A man who combines gentle birth or rank with chivalrous qualities; 2) A man whose conduct conforms to a high standard or propriety of correct behavior; 3) a man of independent means who does not engage in any occupation or profession for gain.

MANHOOD IS
PRICELESS

GMC

CHAPTER 1:

THE REASONS FOR THE REASONS

So, you want to play? Let's talk about that. A lie doesn't care who tells it, but the TRUTH does. A known liar can actually tell you the truth one day, but does it really mean that much coming from him/her? Not really, because you'll expect them to be right back at it tomorrow! A reliable source of the truth, that's what The GMC aims to be. I myself am an advocate for the truth while being a man who loves, fully respects, and adores women. That's normally not the combination you get in today's breed of man. But, here I stand. For the most part I kept my wording tasteful throughout this book. Although, I still managed to use words you may not like or approve of. For example, I could surely use the proper terms for the male and female genitalia. But, we're not just talking about a penis or vagina here. We're grown, right? And, contrary to popular belief thirty is not the new twenty. It seems as though fifteen is. Some fifteen year olds can curse better than I can. Yes, that's a problem. So, just know that the contents of this book have been worded in ways to get a point across clearly. "I want some vagina". That sounds like a joke to me and I'm not trying to be funny. This isn't medical school.

The opinions stressed in my book are what I believe in and what I live by.

IF YOU CAN'T PRACTICE WHAT YOU PREACH, THAT OBVIOUSLY MAKES YOU A HYPOCRITE. YOU ARE ACTUALLY THE WORST OF THE WORST, NO MATTER HOW WELL YOU SPEAK IT. THERE ARE A LOT OF EXCEPTIONAL MEN IN TODAY'S SOCIETY, BUT LIKE ANY HEALTHY BODY OF WORK, THERE IS A CANCER AMONG US. IF YOU CAN'T SPEAK YOUR OWN MIND AND HEART, THAT MAKES YOU A GOOD ACTOR. BE A SOURCE OF INFORMATION, NOT JUST ENTERTAINMENT. KNOWLEDGE IS PRICELESS, SO STRIVE TO LEARN SOMETHING EVERYDAY. EVEN IF YOU ARE IN THE "HOOD" LEARN SOMETHNG NEW ABOUT THE "HOOD" EVERYDAY. MAYBE YOU WILL LEARN A WAY OUT. OBTAIN KNOWLEDGE AND SPREAD YOUR WEALTH. TO ALL THE CANCEROUS MEN WHO DON'T STRIVE TO BECOME RESPECTABLE MEN IN TODAY'S SOCIETY, I DO NOT WISH YOU TO STAY DORMANT. DEVELOP A NEED TO BECOME A BETTER MAN AND ACTIVATE YOURSELF, AND LET THE CHEMOTHERAPY BEGIN!

What's my inspiration and motive for writing this book? I have a need to see women in good situations, and I'll NEVER consider that a downfall. Women have been losing for quite some time now. Before women's suffrage came along, one would be correct in saying women were treated as inferiors due to social laws and traditions of that era. Fast forward to 2011, and that blame can be placed upon a number of things. And I for one, I choose to concentrate on women, and I'll thoroughly explain why throughout this book. Accountability and responsibility are two key ingredients in the recipe for adulthood. I'll explain how these two words are MISSING as I breakdown my thoughts on men and women, and how we interact with one another. I have a need to SIMPLIFY things. When you can just take into consideration the basic responsibilities we have to OURSELVES when engaging in relationships, I guarantee you it will all make more sense. And, that's how this book was written. It is a short read, SIMPLE, to the point, and very informative. We are individuals and none of our situations are the same, but there are similar reasons as to why a lot of us have the same outcomes that we were not hoping to have! It has become the norm to date at will based on what we like and want. Not what we actually need, but what we think is the best way for us to have fun. Well, you can clearly see the disastrous state that the social scene is in. The MAIN problem is women are not considering the circumstances. They are not actually considering the GAME. The game has become a way of life. Let's see who we can have sex with, using the least amount of effort. That has become the mindset of most young men growing up today. It's a game. That's the dating scene today. But, who's suffering the most? Obviously, it is women. I think if women have a clear explanation of what the game is and how it works, then they could possibly delay it. In fact, delay it for life if she so pleases. If you are truly ready for love and all it has to offer, then there are some simple truths you have to take into consideration first.

When asked what makes a woman a good woman, my answer, along with the majority of men is very simple. It is HER SELF RESPECT. Everything else seems to fall into place when self respect is intact for a woman. You often hear women themselves say a woman should never sacrifice her dignity, and self respect. But, there is one thing I have never heard a woman say. And it's the one thing I think so many women are guilty of today. A GOOD WOMAN SHOULD NOT SACRAFICE HER RIGHT TO HAVE A GOOD MAN! Now, you may have heard women say "I deserve a good man". But, let's be honest. Even women who cheat and lie think they deserve a good man, while they remain the woman who cheats and lies. There are also women who THINK they are respecting themselves. Who THINK they are playing it safe when it comes to relationships. Who also think they can behave as a man does. But, when trying to attract a good man, it doesn't matter what you think of yourself. You may know that you're a good woman, but is that his perception of you? Is that really the vibe you are giving? A lot of women want to do things that make them feel safe, and totally disregard what a man thinks. "Take me as I am" is her motto.

When it comes to this state of emergency today's social climate is in, I previously mentioned that I focus on women more. I do so for one reason. WOMEN HAVE THE POWER. A lot of men won't admit to that, or simply won't agree. Well, almost everything that a man does has the influence of a woman behind it. Some of these guys out here would not even be bathing if it weren't for a woman. I myself like to look in the mirror and like what I see. I like to smell good. I like nice clothes. But, we do it for women. I don't care if Jim, Tyrone, and Mike don't approve of my haircut, my clothes, and my style. If Michelle, Kim, and Tonya like it, then I'm cool. The things we do as men, we ultimately do it to please women. The list of things men do to please women goes on and on. So, once again I say women have the power. Men have the ability to manipulate that power. WHEN THE RIGHT WOMAN LOSES HER SELF RESPECT, THE WRONG MAN WILL TAKE ADVANTAGE OF IT.

We have basically become a nation of people who like to live in the moment. We want what we like and we want it now. We have turned the American dream into a fantasy we can make happen today. Never mind what it will cost us tomorrow, next week, or next year. If someone tells you that you can have a big pretty house to live in at this very moment, it's hard to walk away from that. Especially if it's a house that you like and would enjoy living in. What they don't tell you is that you can't afford it and you will have to put in more time, work, and patience until you can. I completely understand how one could not resist that offer. But, it's still an irresponsible thing to do. That's basically the story behind the housing market crash. When responsibility to one's self is lost, someone can easily take advantage of you. That's the game that the banks played with the American public. Well, guess what? When you lose responsibility in regards to your body and feelings, someone will easily take advantage of that also. As individuals we are responsible for our own happiness. In a relationship we chose to share that responsibility with a significant other and trust that they take it as serious as we do. But, when we don't put in the work, time, and patience in our relationships they crash just as the housing market did. Divorces and useless relationships is what we saw happening all around us. Quick marriages and easy move-ins. All because we saw someone we liked and wanted them that instant. Let's bypass the work needed to make this a happy home and get right to what makes this a happy moment. Ultimately you will have to decide whether you want to partake in these games people play or not. If those people who bought those homes had an understanding of the game the banks where playing, do you think they may have made a more educated decision? What if women took into consideration the reasons behind the games that men play? Do you think they would be more responsible with their bodies and minds? Sure, everybody suffered during the housing disaster. But, the banks still got off with a lot easier than the public did. Are men getting off easy during these times of failed relationships? Men suffer from the game as well, but it's sure not as detrimental to us as it is for women.

So, what should men and women expect to get from reading this book? For men, if you are serious about upholding the title of manhood, this book should just be a "head nodder" for you. This book should be confirmation, because the truth will be on display throughout every page. Some of you should learn more than you thought you knew about manhood. I won't get into the actual transformation of boys to men, but I will the transformation of boyfriend to husband. But, we already know the story with men. Some of you will just be reminded. Some of you will be exposed. As for women, the one thing I want you to realize upon completing this book is simple. A woman's self respect is the key to success in regards to finding a good man. You cannot achieve that goal without it. The slightest disregard for this rule can, and has caused women a world of trouble. Some of you have sacrificed your right to have a good man, along with self respect, and that's cool. That's only cool if you don't complain about your man or men in general. But, since so many of you do, let's find out what you have done to your rights, and how do you take them back! If you are a woman who enjoys a lot of random dick, then hopefully this book will just be an interesting read for you. The love for dick you have conquers your need to have a good man, or to be a good woman. Therefore, you should not be complaining. Yet and still, we hear a lot of the "highly active" women complaining about men, too. The Bible should be your ONLY book of choice. You know who you are, but I'm glad you are reading along with us.

In the chapters to come, you will mainly read about these three things: The double standard that exists between men and women, and how it applies to relationships; the "game" that men and women play amongst each other. And, by game I mean the tricks used, the advantages taken, and the premeditated plans men and women have for each other. The third thing is how some women unknowingly have relinquished self respect. I'll explain this by simply explaining how men think.

Delay of Game

Steve Harvey is my idol. His book "Act Like A Lady, Think Like A Man" is a great book I'm sure. I've met a lot of women who have read it, and made references to it and asked my opinion. I didn't read it because I wanted to make sure I formed my own opinions, and didn't want to be labeled a "Steve Harvey" type of guy. Although, I have not been able to avoid that label from some, it's not one to be upset about. I do have an autographed copy of Steve's book that I purchased when I met him. What can I say, we both love women and love to see them doing well, and we take manhood seriously. Ladies, there are many men out here who have the same mentality as I do. I didn't mention Mr. Harvey for any other reason than him being my idol. Great choice on my behalf! With the exception of the three month rule, and the actual title, I know I would pretty much agree with everything he wrote. I don't believe in putting a time table on sex, because it could very well take longer than three months to get comfortable with a person. I don't agree with the title for one simple reason. Men and women can't think like each other. We have fundamental differences which make us desire one another. There are just some things we have to accept about the opposite sex, quit trying to understand them, and just make sound decisions according to those differences. The one thing men know to be true is that women are simply more emotional than we are. Yet, this is the one thing men tend to forget! Fellas, stop asking why your woman cares about certain things ten times more than you do. She can't help it, so just accept that. Accept it, deal with, and make your woman happy if this is the woman you want in your life. I didn't say for you to be a punk. But, realizing that your woman needs you to let her emotions be displayed will save you from a lot of arguments.

Now, before we really get started, let me say I'm not trying to tell anyone how their relationship should go. YOU are the one who has to live with the consequences, so make your own decisions. We all may seek advice from a close friend, or just another person we feel is knowledgeable and can help us. We are all individuals with individual circumstances, so what works for me may not work for you. This book is simply stating some of the harsh truths we ALL have seem to forgotten at times. Many people have never known or took into consideration what actually goes on out here in these social scenes where relationships begin. And, by simply knowing what you're getting into, it makes it so much easier to accept RESPONSIBILITY for the parts we play when things don't go our way. My disclaimer for this book is I'm not knocking anything another ADULT chooses to stand for. If you're pimping, hoing, scheming, tricking, or whatever, just be good at it. Most importantly, take FULL responsibility for it. I just want women to know that no matter what plans a man has for you, they don't go well unless you participate in them of course. We hear women who claim they don't need a man and men aren't shit, but it is VERY rare to hear a man say he doesn't need a woman. Women are surely being exploited and disrespected in more ways than one today, but men don't dismiss the fact that we need them. In my opinion, women have to make better decisions to determine whether she is needed one time, sometimes, a long time, or all the time. And, if you are a woman who is satisfied with being a one time or sometime girl just be prepared to suffer the consequences.

GMC

CHAPTER 2:

GAMETIME

So once again, why do I choose to focus on women more so than men? Well, I have already stated that women have the power. But, they are not using that power to their advantage. It is very obvious that men have to do better. The way women are portrayed and degraded these days is disgusting. Preaching to men and encouraging them to become better men in today's society is certainly a great thing. But, let me ask you a question. A man who has no job, no education, or isn't a good father is still a male. Does this man say to himself, "I have no education, no job, and I'm not a good father, so I don't deserve to have sex with a woman"? No, he doesn't. There are still women sleeping with these dudes. IF IT DIDN'T TAKE MUCH TO GET YOU, A MAN WILL DO EVEN LESS TO KEEP YOU. So, why don't these women who are sleeping with no good men tell him he doesn't deserve her? There are various answers to this question. Some are desperate. Some just don't want to be alone. But, what that all boils down to is, they have sacrificed their right to have a good man.

There are two groups of people that make up the social scene we have today. People that are playing the game, and people that are not. The worst thing that's happening to women right now is that she is normally the one not wanting to play, but has feelings for a man who does. The saddest thing about the game is the ones who don't know they are playing it. That's where the shock and disappointment comes from when a relationship suddenly goes downhill. Again, what is the "game"? The game is the chess match men and women play. The game consists of people who don't have the other's best interest at heart. In the past, there was only the pimp game, which actually had three components. Those three things are the pimp, trick, and the prostitute. That game was based on money, and fueled by the thirst for it. People involved in this type of lifestyle had clear cut goals, which is to buy or sell sex. Why do I even mention the pimp game? I mean, there is no mistaking those involved, right? Pimps are not shy about what they do, and neither are prostitutes. So, what effect could this game have on you while trying to find a significant other? Well, the pimp game's tactics and methods became a part of the dating scene. Even when the average Joe, or lamest rapper can get a few women on his team, he may refer to himself as a pimp or player. First, let me explain the reasons behind the game.

The easiest way to subdue a person's mind is to belittle them. When someone is being "pimped", that means they basically have been convinced to think and act a certain way, and do things they may not have normally done. And, it is usually the most beneficial to the person who is doing the pimping. In case you didn't know, there are pimps in almost every line of work you can imagine today. Somebody is taking advantage of somebody. Somebody is telling a person(s) that what they are doing is what's best for them, when actually it's not. People are being pimped in churches, their jobs, and their own homes. We are talking about the dating scene right now, and how these same tactics are used by men and women with devious motives and intentions.

Now, it's hard for me to imagine that women began to call themselves bitches, whores, sluts, etc. Unless, the first female pimps were lesbians, it's safe to say that these are all terms that men created. These are terms that are used to belittle women. And to this day, they reign supreme. The one thing women need to realize is; THIS GAME WAS DESIGNED FOR WOMEN TO LOSE. All you women who want to label yourselves as players, female pimps, or whatever. You are still losers. The main objective of the game is to create ways for a man to obtain sex from a woman. Love and affection have no place in this game. A woman may very well be getting a man to give her money, or buy her gifts and all that. But, is she giving away her body? Men don't care how much it cost, especially if he can afford it. When a woman puts a cheap price on something that is supposed to be priceless, the right man will find her. Her womanhood should only be paid for by manhood. My manhood is priceless. So, if a woman rewards a man with her womanhood, which is priceless, it should mean that he paid for it with his manhood. That's two people holding each other to respectable standards as a grown woman and man. Today, sex is rewarded because you are attractive, or how much money you have, or simply selling a dream. Sex these days is rewarded strictly by word of mouth on some occasions. A man's reputation can get him the green light from some women.

I strongly urge women to just be themselves to get a man. Leave the games alone, and just be a woman at all times. I know it gets hard out here, and the selection of quality men has dropped dramatically. One thing I do know is that men do whatever it takes to get the woman he wants. If you desire a man in your life, you first have to have the desire to be a woman.

And, if you are a person who doesn't agree that the dating and pimp game are now intertwined, ask yourself this. How did the average Joe walking the streets, or even the average rapper on television get to the point where it was cool to label themselves a "pimp"? We hear and see it all the time. Soon as a guy feels he is dating women at his own will, he's now a pimp and a player. Nowadays, the criteria for being a pimp is money, cars, and nice clothes. You don't have to know a thing about women and never have had to put in work on the track. My money and cars enables me to have sex with a lot of women, so I'm pimpin! Or, once a guy has managed to get a couple of women to go on DATES with him, he's pimpin! When a woman goes out on a date with more than one man within a week or so, she's a ho. So I ask you, is it only a figment of my imagination when I say pimpig, hoing, and dating are all one of the same? Courting a woman and chivalry have almost become laughable acts these days. That's a shame. Concentrating on ONE man or woman at a time is considered to be lame. I don't know about you, but I would welcome back the days of knowing who's really pimping and hoing, or simply looking to go out on a nice date. How can we distinguish between the two? We simply do the things pimps and hos don't like. Operate with honesty and respect when choosing someone to date. Can you do that? It's called being grown. Yeah, a lot of you claim to be. But, I don't just mean your eighteenth birthday. I'm talking about responsibility, respect, integrity, honesty, and all those words that a Vegas pimp would slap a bitch for. She got some nerves for having self respect, doesn't she?

CHAPTER 3:

SO YOU WANT TO BE A PLAYER

First, let's talk about the people who are still playing the game. As I mentioned before, love, affection, and all their synonyms have NO PLACE in the game. The most important thing to know, if you choose to play is this: You can't play the game and hate the game. That makes you lame to the game.

Fellas, if your woman doesn't know you are a player then that makes you a LIAR. Players don't lie. Players play and could care less who's watching. Cheating is for cowards. There will come a time when you encounter a woman who makes you want to tell the truth. But, you'll be so scared to reveal the real you to the point where all you do is lie. It's what you do best. Although I believe in monogamy, I'm not one to criticize anyone who doesn't. I've juggled women before, and I learned quickly that I could still do it with the truth. That didn't make me a man, though. Any fool can have sex as long as he/she finds another fool. Hopefully, there will come a time when being honest with yourself will force you to be truthful with others. Manhood has no age minimum. It is a state of mind and a matter of execution. You may think you are the player of all players, but just know this- the game will get tired of you at some point. It's unavoidable. You can't delay becoming a respectable man forever.

Some people want to play, but can't handle their losses. When you are a person who is not ready for a serious relationship but still wants to have sex, you are a participant. Like it or not, you are a part of the game! Have you ever wondered how can a person be so heartless and inconsiderate towards you? Because your feelings got involved, and became more important than the game you are playing. The one thing so many people, normally WOMEN, don't realize is crucial. And, that is if you don't want a relationship, then your feelings and emotions have to be put away in places of your body that are not your heart or your mind. We all know WOMEN are the more EMOTIONAL human beings by nature. So, please understand that this is not what you need, but so many women choose to play. If you want feelings of true love and affection to prevail, then DON'T PLAY! HONESTY IS SO SEXY TO THE PEOPLE WHO ARE LOOKING FOR IT, believe me.

Now, how did the "pimp" game infiltrate the dating scene? Well, not every man was a good pimp, and not every woman was a good whore. So, there are still men and women who want sex, right? There are men and women who don't want a commitment, right? And, there are men and women who don't want to break the law. Yes, that's funny. The actual pimp game was based on sex and money. The dating game has become a cat and mouse game based on sex and money, combined with the play on emotions. And, just like the pimp game, there have been tactics used to belittle women. Sex and money are actually used as tools to control one's emotions. Also, the same type of degrading terms created in the pimp game have been created in the dating game as well. But, men also have their own negative titles on these dating scenes. The dating scene can consist of gold diggers, home wreckers, sideline whores, sugar daddies, a plan B, and a host of other characters. You can go to your local dine-in restaurant and identify all of the previous mentioned on most occasions. I can remember a time when a date actually was a thing used to get to know a person you wanted a monogamous relationship with. These days, people go on dates to see what they can get out of that person. Some are just looking for sex (normally men), money, or quite simply a free meal perhaps. And, the play on emotions to acquire these things is what has so many people's lives in turmoil. People lie and deceive each other in so many ways. You have men who lie about what they want and who they are. Men play on a woman's emotions, being that they are so emotional. Again, WOMEN HAVE THE POWER, but the smallest sign of self respect being lost gives that man the power to manipulate. Yes, I keep referring to women as EMOTIONAL. Some fellas have a confused look on their face when a woman has flipped. She's EMOTIONAL. How can we forget this?

The dating scene has become a place to witness selfless acts. I just mentioned that a woman who shows the slightest sign of a weakness will be manipulated by the wrong man. When you both are in it for something real, then your weaknesses will be embraced in the right way. I'll explain that at a later time, but right now we are talking about these sharks in the water.

Whatever happened to CHIVALRY? Chivalry is important because it will enable a lot of women to avoid a man they have no business dating. Is chivalry dead? No, I don't think it is, but I do think a lot of women have lowered their standards. I have seen cases where chivalry actually embarrasses some women. Some women are just too "independent". Some women just have never been taught to demand it, or have forgotten. But, since the dating scene has basically become an act these days, you can't rely on chivalry alone to judge a man's character. A man with bad intentions can pull out all the tricks, including chivalry. So many women ask me how to recognize a man who is trying to run game on them. Well, the signs will be there. The thing I see most women being guilty of is having a short term memory. Women are more forgiving than men, I understand that. I mentioned chivalry because it should NEVER stop. Some women will forget what a man has done wrong, as soon as he does something right. Should it matter that chivalry is on FULL display for you tonight, when you know he was probably displaying it for another woman yesterday? No, it shouldn't, because you shouldn't even be there! Unless, you are a woman who has accepted the "sideline" or "plan b" role, you shouldn't be so forgiving.

The sad thing is a woman in this position has no clue if she is a plan B, C, or maybe even D. Some women say that they don't care as long as they are getting what they want. That could be money, or even just sex is what I hear most these women say. For all of you who have this mentality, unless you plan on living the rest of your life this way, you can't afford this. Your RESPECT in society is slowly dwindling away day by day living this lifestyle. And, soon you may find out how much self respect you have lost the instant you try to find a respectful man. THE DOUBLE STANDARD IS IN FULL EFFECT in these situations. Men can jump in and out of this game because men don't care. Men don't operate on emotions like women do. Any adult should know this to be true.

Ah, the double standard. The double standard is what so many women REFUSE to respect, and it causes so much trouble in their life. "WHY CAN A MAN HAVE SO MANY SEX PARTNERS, BUT A WOMAN CAN'T?" This is the question so many women still feel the need to ask. Ok, let me say that I understand why women say that this double standard isn't fair. Men who have sex with a lot of women are called players, pimps, womanizers, and at worst a dog. The title "man-whore" isn't even detrimental to a man's reputation. That man can still find him a respectable woman when he is ready to do so. THAT'S JUST LIFE.

Some women think they can behave as a man does when it comes to the dating scene and relationships in general. WRONG. A woman can't behave as a man does and maintain the respect level she needs in today's society. So many women fail to realize that the double standard is there to PROTECT women. Protect them from what you might ask? Protect them from being labeled as "hos" and "sluts", and every other thing a woman may not liked to be called. Let me explain how it protects you women with this example: I like to use the kissing analogy when women ask me about the double standard. If two women kiss, nobody will label them as lesbians. Actually, that may get a round of applause from the majority of people. On the other hand, what if two men kiss? What two men, who are not gay, actually kiss? Kissing is an act that will surely get two men the gay label. MEN RESPECT THIS DOUBLE STANDARD and have no problem with it. This is very simple for men. If you don't want to be labeled as gay, then SIMPLY DON'T KISS other men. Now, ladies please apply that to you having sex with a lot of men. If you don't want to be labeled as a "ho", then you should simply NOT HAVE SEX WITH A LOT OF MEN. No matter how hard you try, there is no way around this double standard, so PLEASE RESPECT IT! Brittany Spears and Madonna kissed live on stage before a worldwide audience. NOT ONE single headline the next day suggested that either one of them was a lesbian. Lil Wayne and Baby also kissed. And, you saw what happened with that situation. I rest my case.

Women also ask me this: What is considered a lot of men to the man I want? There is an unusual answer to this question, but it is so very true. And, the answer is how many of them does he know personally. How many of these past sex partners might he encounter on a daily basis? It is very rare that a man will enter a serious relationship with, let alone marry, a woman he knows all the homeys has been with. That's just a natural insecurity that men have. Yes, there are some men out there who will, and we call them LAME. The type of man who will take on the town whore is normally the man who is not a respectful person to begin with. No, he is not just a sweet, forgiving, considerate man. He is just lame, or more than likely has bad intentions for that woman. Or, it could simply be she is the only woman who would have him, because he will have her. Does a relationship that consists of two "whores" who are still out there set a good example of a good relationship? No, because they are normally bad parents and create turmoil for others. Those types of relationships are entertaining at times, but still such a sad story. That's the type of stuff you see on The Maury Povich Show. Do you really want to be involved with a relationship that lands you a spot on there?

Some women feel that the "ho" title gets tossed around unfairly. I'm well aware that good people sometimes make bad decisions. We are only human. The only time I have a problem with people making bad decisions is when they don't want to be held responsible for them. Or, when they try to pass the decision off as a mistake and didn't learn from them. LADIES, IT ONLY TAKES ONE "HO" ACT TO GET YOU THE "HO" LABEL. This is often the case for women who sleep with men who are already involved. For numerous reasons, men still manage to manipulate a GOOD woman to sleep with them while he's involved. Not all of the women are good women of course. Some are just trifling women who love to sleep with somebody's boyfriend/husband. But, what about the woman who was lied to and deceived by the man? She is simply a victim. There are also women who may sleep with a man on the first date, or after a couple of dates, and don't want the "ho" title. Let me ask you all something. Let's say there is a person who has went to the police station and snitched on somebody. And, that is that person's first time ever snitching and they never did it again. Does the fact that he/she never did it again NOT make them a snitch? No, it doesn't. So, a woman who sleeps with a man on the first date is considered a "ho" by the vast majority of men. I don't care what a man may tell you, and I guess I'm snitching right now, because I'm telling you we consider that a "ho" move. And, for the woman who has never slept with another woman's boyfriend/ husband, but does it one time. She will get the "ho" title. Normally, the title that woman gets is courtesy of the woman who's man she slept with. When a woman finds out about her man sleeping with another woman, do kind words on her behalf come to mind? Does that woman say "that nice respectable woman slept with my man"? No, it's usually that bitch, slut, whore, etc., slept with my man. But hey, the woman actually can be a nice respectable woman, who just happened to make a bad decision and slept with the wrong man. So, sometimes it's just who actually knows the woman and her past as I mentioned before. The man who does know the woman who slept with him or another man on the first date may call her a "ho". The woman who slept with another woman's man may get the "ho" title, but she feels it is unfair. Again, it only takes one "ho" act to be seen as a "ho" in some people's eyes. I don't think there is NOTHING a man can do to earn a woman's body in one night. Do you? I've heard women who do think this is OK and claim that they are just comfortable with their sexuality, or just having fun. They actually want to tip toe around the game and don't realize they are already in it.

So again, understand that if you are not seeking a monogamous relationship, then you are a part of the game. It is a high possibility that you will get played. Can you handle it? Can you take a loss like a man? Can you dust yourself off like a big girl and not cry? Apparently not because all I see is men losing in court rooms and complaining about it, and women crying all over the place.

CHAPTER 4:

GIRLS JUST WANNA HAVE FUN

WOMEN HAVE TO MUCH TO LOSE while trying to succeed in this game. I have heard way too many women say "I'm just having fun" with these men. That quote is normally the purr of a young kitten, or the roar of a cougar. Young women in their teens, and some throughout their twenties, tend to have this mentality. Or, like a young man, a young lady may just want to get it out of her system. This mentality can mean a few hardships for a young man and pure hell for a young woman. Due to the DOUBLE STANDARD, this lifestyle will be far more detrimental to her reputation than it will his. If this were not true, women would not be asking the questions that I mentioned earlier. Questions such as why are men considered pimps and players when they sleep with a lot of women, but women are whores when they sleep with a lot of men? Another quote that I often hear women say is "I have my needs". When a woman says that, it means she knows she may have slept with a man she wasn't supposed to, but her "needs" were more important at the time. SHE SACRAFICED HER RIGHT TO HAVE A GOOD MAN. Her need for sex became more important than having an honest, loving, caring, man, and every other "good" word you can think of. Good in bed is the only thing a woman is looking for to satisfy those "needs" she speaks of. There is no other logical way to look at that. So, are those really needs a woman is talking about when she uses that quote? No, that is simply a "want" that she has satisfied. I know we all can get lonely while living the single life. But, loneliness is only a state of mind. Just call it what is. You just got HORNY! There are actually some respectable women who will use this EXCUSE to sleep with a man. And, they will use that quote "I have my needs". But, while living the single life and satisfying her "needs", SHE SACRAFICED HER RIGHT TO HAVE A GOOD MAN. Yes, men in the game love women who jut have "needs". So, what happens if she gets pregnant while satisfying her needs? Or, the EMOTIONAL creature she is by nature takes over? Pure hell is what happens. Pure hell is what we see caused by men and women who failed to respect the game they were playing in.

A popular label used in the game is "FRIENDS WITH BENEFITS". A lot of women will use this "friend" to satisfy her "needs". Before I get into this ridiculous "friends with benefits" title, let me define the word friend as it is in the dictionary.

FRIEND: 1) A PERSON KNOWN WELL TO ANOTHER AND REGARDED WITH LIKING, AFFECTION, AND LOYALTY. If you look at the history of the word friend, it is described as *a LOVER, LITERALLY.*

FRIENDS DON'T HAVE SEX. The definition of the word friends does not refer to anything SEXUAL. I have men in my life that I love. The word friend can be used to describe the relationship between any gender, and not just a man and a woman. The men that I love, I don't want to have sex with! So I ask, why do people who have sex feel the need to put a "friends" title on their relationship sometimes? Because, the word "friends" is the way to stay away from a possible commitment! It is a way to excuse LOYALTY. The word "friend" is more misused than the word love these days. "Friends with benefits" is a man's dream, and a woman's nightmare. Sometimes, she just never realizes the nightmare she is in until she wakes up screaming because her "friend" has hurt her so. I know it's easy to refer to someone as our friend. The word has become a common way to introduce someone to others. But it still has to fit the true description of what that person is to you, and often times it doesn't.

In most cases, a woman has not realized the monster she is creating in a man. If you agree to just be "friends" with a man you are having sex with, you are literally inserting his penis into a vagina that isn't yours. What happens in these situations is a woman relieves a man of damn near ALL responsibilities to her. NONE OF US CAN CONTROL NATURAL EMOTIONS. Jealousy, envy, or simply becoming attached are things you cannot control. What we have control over is the decisions we make due to these emotions and feelings. And, we ALL have become attached to a person we said we would not fall for. When emotions are running high, ESPECIALLY for women, sound decision making is not a strong point. Broken windows, the vandalizing of personal property, and even murder is evidence of these acts of jealousy and mixed emotions I speak of. We see it and read about it every day. Somebody's "friend" keyed their car, showed up at their job, or tried to kill them. So, for anybody who has a problem with the definition of the word friend that I just gave, don't dispute me, dispute history and the people who write the dictionaries. That would be Webster and company.

So, we have the woman who is getting her "needs" satisfied by her "friend", and the man who has a job that is to basically be friendly. But, what if he acquires another "friend"? After all, nobody is supposed to be getting attached in this "friendship", right? So now he meets another nice young lady who is ok with the two of them just being "friends" and, possibly meets another one as well. Now, this same young man is having sex with multiple "friends". He is the guy who is called a dog, and he has bitches, his females. Actually, other than just being irresponsible, he has done nothing wrong. But, nobody is supposed to be getting attached to anyone, right? So, who really has the problem with these situations? The man certainly doesn't. Women may say they don't care if he sleeps with other women, but they often do. Remember, those emotions can only stay tucked away for so long! What normally happens when she finds out? Well, I don't have to tell you again, because we've all heard the stories. She either does something drastic fueled by her emotions, or she simply breaks it off with the man who is now no good in her eyes. And worst case, she seeks revenge by acquiring another "friend" herself, and a "ho" is born. Is it cool to cheat because your mate cheated on you?

Well, how can you progress as a human being if you lower yourself to the level of the person that wronged you? And once again, in this situation, did anyone actually cheat?

So, where is the benefit for the woman? Is sex all she gets? Is that worth it? She most definitely gets to stare the DOUBLE STANDARD right in its face again. While he is being a player and a pimp with his "friends", the woman gets to be a "whore" with hers. In these situations, the woman has SACRAFICED HER RIGHT TO HAVE A GOOD MAN just to be a man's "friend". Bottom line, stop expecting a man to be your friend and nothing more. That is against the laws of nature. Men are SUPPOSED to be attracted to women. Nobody is exempt from the laws of nature.

Out of these situations we are getting a lot of disasters and lives that are made that much harder to live. Even though everybody involved may have been honest with each other, they were not honest with THEMSELVES. These "friends" are producing single mothers, single parent homes, the passing of STD's, and a host of other things bringing down our communities. What this means is society as a whole is not being responsible enough to continue on with these types of relationships, no matter how much FUN they may be! Open relationships are not something I recommend, but to each his/her own, right? Just be ready to hold YOURSELF accountable and responsible for ALL consequences. But, this is not the case today. So many people want to complain about the outcomes and repercussions, while not holding themselves responsible for them. You shouldn't complain about your "baby mama" or "baby daddy" when you had no business sleeping with your "friend". There are people who actually take the time to choose a person to engage in a real relationship with. And, even when they don't work out, we don't see the same problems and heartbreak we see with the ones who are just having fun. And just so you know, I used quotation marks around the word "friends" a lot in hopes that you would get tired of seeing them. That's just how much I'm tired of hearing the word being misused.

I say women have too much to lose because it is true. Men can't bear children. Men don't have to worry so much about their reputation on the social scene. Men are not insulted when you call them a whore. In most cases, it's a compliment. Dick being thrown around doesn't lose its shine like a pussy does. Pussy being thrown around becomes a garbage can that dicks can be thrown in, pulled out, and cleaned off. You can put a garbage bag (condom) in the garbage can, but it's still a garbage can. Ladies, don't let a man throw trash in you. Make him put something in their worth recycling (reproducing), or at least try to stick with one garbage man!

Open relationships. This is another title some people like to throw around for the sake of having fun. Are they really that fun? First of all, what man agrees to let other men sleep with HIS woman? A weak one, maybe? Or, how about a damn fool? No man can be at all serious about a woman he allows back into his home with numerous DNA samples on and in her body. If the only way you and a person can stay together is by allowing other sexual partners, just accept the fact that you're both whores. There's nothing wrong with being a whore until you can't admit to it. Open relationships work because the doors of the clinic and church are always open. Those are two places you can go to get your openness forgiven or forgotten.

Ladies, I'm sorry. Well, actually I'm not. Fun for you just simply cannot be centered around sex. No, it shouldn't be for men either. But again, men can bounce back from these disasters much, much easier than a woman can. That's the part that's not so fun to go through but fun for others to watch or exploit. Talk shows, all the judge shows, are simply the result of friends with benefits and open relationships. The majority of the couples you see on those shows were people who just wanted to have fun. These situations get exploited by divorce lawyers and the court system. As long as people continue to have babies by their friends the child support system will keep prospering along with divorce lawyers. People want to play and are afraid of putting in real work for a real relationship. Happy families and fewer divorces are not going to become common again as long as "friends with benefits" and "open relationships" are considered relationships. They are fronts. They are fronts for people who just don't want to commit.

Women are just too valuable and relinquish too much power while engaging in these types of situations. Your egos, self esteem, and reputation suffer blows that some women never recover from. A very important thing I want women to realize is that men are not going to stop playing these games as long as women participate in them. These days, a man will leave his wife because she gained weight. As her better half it's his job to keep her up in every way, as is hers to him. If your woman has "let herself go" then you helped her. You both gained weight. So, deal with it fellas. It's easy for men to leave women for a reason such as weight gain because he can go find a slim one that wants to have fun. No work required. It's gotten to a point where men expect to get pussy with the least amount of work possible. And, that's been an expectation fulfilled and made possible by too many women.

CHAPTER 5:

I DON'T WANNA BE A PLAYER NO MORE

This chapter and those after it are for the men and women who are SERIOUS about having a monogamous relationship. There are people who have developed a NEED, not a want, to have one. But, once again, I'm primarily talking to women. Women are the ones who are in a state of emergency when it comes to relationships.

Before you even think about engaging in a new relationship, you need to be TOTALLY HONEST WITH YOURSELF. If you know you are STILL the type of person who likes to sleep around, please do that. IT'S NORMALLY MEN who have difficulty admitting when they are not relationship material. As you all should know, a relationship is hard work. If real love is what you desire, that takes an enormous amount of dedication.

IF YOU WANT SOMETHING PURE, THAT MEANS YOU HAVE TO COMBINE SOMETHING PURE, WITH SOMETHING ELSE THAT IS PURE AS WELL. SO IN ORDER TO GET PURE LOVE, THAT'S WHAT YOU NEED TO BRING TO THE TABLE. THE INSTANT YOU CONTAMINATE YOUR LOVE, IT CAN NEVER GO BACK TO BEING PURE. If your mate doesn't know about the dirt you have done, does that not still make it dirt? Don't expect your relationship to work if you have contaminated it. That "what they don't know won't hurt them" line is bull. Even dirt under the rug still exists.

One simple thing that has gotten all of us in trouble at one point in time is a CRUSH. There are some of us who actually strive to have a monogamous relationship. But, there is always a person who catches your attention. I wanted to talk about that a little bit.

CRUSHES ARE NORMAL. WHEN IN A RELATIONSHIP, WHAT YOU THOUGHT WAS ATTRACTIVE TO YOU DOESN'T BECOME UNATTRACTIVE BECAUSE YOU ARE INVOVLED. BUT, IT'S NOT OK WHEN DAMN NEAR EVERYBODY YOU SEE STARTS LOOKING BETTER THAN YOUR MATE TO YOU. AT THIS POINT, YOU ARE IN DENIAL. AND NOW THAT CRUSH BECOMES TEMPTATION. THIS is when THE BOYS AND GIRLS GET SEPERATED FROM THE GROWN MEN AND WOMEN. DON'T DO THINGS JUST BECAUSE YOU CAN.

So basically what I'm saying is leave your mate because they make you unhappy, not because you THINK someone you met will make you happier.

So, what happens when we tell ourselves that we are through with the games? That point when a man or woman realizes that they want something real. When love, affection, trust, loyalty, and all the other things that makes for a good relationship is what you are ready to give and receive. How do we accomplish that? Some people get discouraged and give up on love, and fall right back into playing games. This relapse may be a result of a person who actually tried, but was hurt, or wasn't patient enough to wait on the right mate. There are some people who just simply love sex too much, and can't see themselves with only one sex partner. Of course, sexual addictions are real. Some people unwillingly put themselves back into the game because they are lonely, but willingly allow a person that they know is not relationship material into their lives. As I stated earlier in this book, a lot of people confuse the word lonely with the word horny. If you want a good relationship and you start to feel lonely, get a pet. And, get a pet that is an actual animal, not a human being. You know what I'm saying.

Once again, why do I choose to focus on women more on relation-ship matters? Because, you all have the power to get what you want.

And, this transition of leaving the game is much easier for a man than it is a woman. Why is it easier for men? Well, that good ole DOUBLE STANDARD shows its face, yet again. I have accepted the fact that there will be women who will never respect this. But, they can't deny that it exists! Often times, I just have to refer to our dictionaries and encyclopedias for help. So, feel free to research what the definition of a double standard is. Let me share with you what I found, and didn't have to refer to any book or website to know it to be true. But I did anyway just to share it with you all.

A DOUBLE STANDARD IS ANY CODE OR SET OF PRINCIPLES CONTAINING DIFFERENT PROVISIONS FOR ONE GROUP OF PEOPLE THAN FOR ANOTHER, ESP. AN UNWRITTEN CODE FOR SEXUAL BEHAVIOR PERMITTING MEN MORE FREEDOM THAN WOMEN.

Being that some people have actually defined what they think a word(s) means during their life, I sometimes just have to give them the real definition. Just as I did with the word FRIENDS earlier in this book, I want people to know what they are saying, and how they are misconstruing certain things to fit their lifestyles. And, let me reiterate that friends don't have sex. But, some people have developed their own definition of a friend and what friends actually do. And, just to fit their lifestyle and feel safe or justify it, the word friend has been conveniently been passed off as a person you are not committed to, but are having sex with. The double standard has not been passed off as anything, but sadly it has not been respected. It is mostly women who have a problem with the double standard because they are the ones who can't have sex freely like men. And, who doesn't enjoy sex, right?

I have mentioned the double standard numerous times. I can't stress enough how important it is for women to respect it. The double standard is for the protection of women, but this is the point in life when it may hurt her the most. When a woman is seeking a mate, does the double standard cause some unfair opinions to be formed about her? Well, a lot of women will certainly agree that it does. In past discussions and debates I have had with women, usually the ones who do have an "active" background think the double standard is unfair. The women who have been considered easy and straight up whores on the dating scene create some major obstacles for themselves, simply because the double standard plays no role on how they carried themselves in the past.

FIRST, LET ME SAY DON'T LET YOUR PAST BE THE REASON YOU ARE SKEPTICAL ABOUT YOUR FUTURE. THERE IS NO NEED TO DWELL ON WHAT YOU COULD HAVE BEEN OR SHOULD HAVE DONE. EMBRACE WHAT YOU CAN BE, AND WHAT YOU WILL BECOME IF YOU TRY.

That goes for men and women on life in general. But, some people's lives have become so complicated due to their sexual behavior alone. And, the truth of the matter is a woman's sexual history can be more detrimental to her image and reputation than a man's can, and that's just life. Life is not fair to those who don't accept the fact that life is going to happen.

When there is a woman that a man can see himself having a future with, her background does play a major role in this situation. I previously mentioned that how much he actually knows basically determines how big of a role it plays. So, any man who chooses to ask a woman about her past is a damn fool. We can't run from our past. You shouldn't have to ask because all your questions will be answered in time. Just pay attention to your woman. Yes, men are just that insecure, but it is a NATURAL insecurity. I mentioned this insecurity that men have, but now let's dig a little deeper. This insecurity protects us from actually having to jump to conclusions. This insecurity is very hard for women to understand, but it's one of those fundamental differences that we should just respect. This insecurity can play a role in determining how we feel about a woman's background and our future with her. Women need to respect this insecurity and understand why the MAJORITY of men don't approve of a woman having male "FRIENDS" while they are in a relationship. The MAJORITY of men don't want to know about your past sexual history, unless we WITNESSED it not involving a lot of men. How often is that the case? Now, this natural insecurity isn't a man's downfall unless, he tries to ignore it. A lot of men will say what sounds good (he doesn't care about his woman's past or if she has male friends). Of course he doesn't want to come off as a jealous or insecure man. In my opinion, when it comes to your mate's past, NEVER ask questions unless the past has presented itself. Those curious questions such as "how many people have you slept with" should just be left alone.

Men are insecure in regards to other men. Men are insecure about other men because we know men. There are too many women who feel like their man is a jealous human being, and feel they should be able to have male "friends" while in a relationship. Please refer back to the definition of the word FRIENDS that I gave you earlier. Can a woman have male colleagues and associates? She most certainly can. The only reason I went into this subject of a man's natural insecurity is because it will cause him to make a judgment on a woman's background that she may not like. One of those may simply be "she likes a lot of men" and will automatically cause him not to trust your judgement. . These "friends" a woman may often have are a part of her past. And, her man will have his own set of motives and ambitions as to why this other man wants to be, and has been her "friend". And, this is something I have a hard time explaining to women who just don't understand why her man isn't too thrilled about her and her male "friends". For any man who disagrees, please let me take your woman out this weekend. We'll go as "friends". You're not invited. Some men actually try to sell the fact that they can have female friends on a platonic level. They do so to make themselves seem like a very secure individual. We'll see how secure you are after a few dinner dates that me and your woman have. She and I will just be "friends" so you have nothing to worry about, right? Maybe one day, she'll ask you if you want to join "us". It's always cool until it's YOUR woman.

There is a way I describe this insecurity that I speak of and I use lions as an example. Of course, I'm not trying to personify lions. But, there is a real similarity between the male human being and the male lion when it comes to how we feel about a female. A male lion has a goal to be the head and sole protector of a pride, which consists of him and female lions. If you have ever watched a pride of lions on television, you will know exactly what I'm talking about. When a male lion that is not a part of the pride comes around or enters their territory, the male lion is the only one who reacts in a PROTECTIVE manner. That's what he is supposed to do.

The females in the pride do not even feel threatened at all. But, that male lion knows that there is a motive and a reason that the other male lion is here. Although, the intruding male lion may not act on any of his motives for whatever reasons, they are still there, and the pride leader knows this to be a POTENTIAL threat. Men don't do things for women just to be doing them. Not saying a man can't generally just be a nice and respectable guy. Any extra effort to become a woman's "friend" has a motive. And, this is what men know to be true. So, while most women feel that their male "friend" poses no threat to her and her relationship, men know better. Ladies, expect your lion to roar and bite the shit out of any potential threat. That's his job. I'm not referring to the lion that accuses you of visiting another pride and doesn't trust you. That's the overprotective guy. Just don't expect your man to be so receptive of male friends. That's not our nature. If he's smiling at your male friends and acting like it's all good, he's simply showing him the teeth.

I mentioned earlier that men and women being just friends is something I think is against the laws of nature. I am a man. I like women. I like women parts. They attract me. I'm certainly not saying a man can't show a woman the upmost respect at all times. That doesn't mean she is not attractive to him, though. I have female colleagues. I have female acquaintances. I do not consider them someone that I would attempt to have sex with one day. But, FRIENDS interact on a personal level on a frequent basis. And, I don't mean your co-workers. That's a forced setting. When two people make an effort to see each other in a neutral non-work related setting, then they are engaged in a relationship. It may not be a sexual relationship, YET. Once friends have sex, they have started a relationship. Can we all agree that a relationship has to start with a friendship first? So, what makes some people think they can toy around with a friendship? All my female friends are related to me. I don't want to have sex with my kin. Do you? Every other female in my life is a colleague. The woman I'm in a relationship with is my friend. If a man and a woman like to refer to themselves as "friends" then there is an attraction on one end, or both. That doesn't mean either of them will ever act on it. But, the fact remains that NOBODY is exempt from the laws of nature. Nature will ALWAYS take its course. It's just a matter of time.

That's not me drawing my own conclusions or making any assumptions. The laws of nature were long decided before you and were born.

Also, JEALOUSY comes into play a lot with relationships. We often become jealous of our mate for the very reasons we were attracted to them. Don't be a guilty of "mate hate". Some relationships never get off the ground because someone was jealous of the attention their mate continues to get. Classic example: A man dating a stripper or exotic dancer. You know very well when you've met someone who is "popular" among the opposite sex. Don't let your jealousy of that fact ruin a potential relationship. Jealousy is a NATURAL emotion that you can't control. What you do have control of is the actions you take because of it. Those actions will determine whether you are a hater, or an admirer. Shouldn't we all admire our mates? Some people can't do that. Instead, they hate to see their mate out in public receiving the very same attention that they gave to him/her themselves. That's jealousy. Of course, this is where trust comes into play.

Why do I even mention this natural insecurity that men have? How does it relate to how a man views a woman's past? It relates because it is one way that tells a man how serious she is about a future with him. How she handles other men will let him know what type of woman he is up against. Men don't like to compete with other men for the woman he wants to build something real with. Pursuing a woman and trying to gain her confidence and trust is one thing, but her allowing other men to dictate her decision is not something men like to deal with. And, women and their nonchalant attitude about other men will push him away, or he may just go along with it to have sex with her.

Now that you are ready to have a real monogamous relationship, there are some key things a woman needs to know that will help her. 1) IF SHE DOESN'T WANT TO BE JUDGED BY HER PAST, THEN SHE NEEDS TO ACKNOWLEDGE IT.

Once again, men are not concerned so much about their own sexual history because it's normally not a deal breaker for a woman. It is very rare that a woman will not be with a man because he has slept with a lot of women. If he is knowingly STILL sleeping with a lot of women, then of course she should let him pass. But, as we all know, that's not always the choice a woman makes. A lot of women think that they are different and that they will "change" a man. If he's still sleeping around, NONE of you are different. A man still playing the "game" sees all women as pussy. Now, unless she has moved to another city, and maybe even another state, a woman simply needs to acknowledge her past. Even then, she's just prolonging the inevitable. YOU CAN'T RUN FROM YOUR PAST. Some women know they have slept with a lot of men, but don't want that to be the topic of discussion at any point in time. Sorry, but it will be one day because your past follows you around longer than a man's does, and will more than likely present itself one day. I can't stress that enough. But, if you are a woman who carries herself as a lady in present times, then there is no need to deny your past. The SURPRISES are what a man does not like. And, if a man worries about what you have done more so than what you are today, then he does not deserve you. The only time a man tries to keep his past a secret is when he is still involved with the past. Other than that, he could care less if you know about every single woman he has slept with. Some women try to keep their past a secret because they are simply ashamed, or there is a man in her past that her new man knows very well. Even in that case, if it comes up, don't deny it. WHAT I DON'T WANT A WOMAN TO DO IS ASSUME WHAT A MAN THINKS ABOUT HER. Some women who know her background is not one of a "good girl" will assume a man wants to treat her as such. Honestly, men don't like or respect ADULT whores. As an adult, we all should understand that the majority of us, men and women, will go through a stage in life when we are more sexually free. We experiment more during out younger years mostly. But, let me state once more that this stage in life can be much more harmful to a young woman than a man. So, what's the excuse for a person who is supposed to be grown? At what age do you not want to be a woman who's just "out there"?

2) DON'T FALL IN LOVE WITH THAT PERSON, FALL IN LOVE WITH THE WAY THAT PERSON LOVES YOU. GOOD SEX AND GOOD LOOKS DOES NOT LEAD TO A GOOD RELATIONSHIP. I said "that person" because this goes for men and women. But, it is normally a woman who falls in love with a man (sex), and not what he actually does for her. If this were not true, then we wouldn't have so many women

allowing a man to stay in her life who she knows doesn't need to be. Good sex is often a blanket that covers a horrible relationship. All kinds of trouble may lie underneath it, and love is nowhere to be found.

Now, I'm not going to go into what I think love is. We are all individuals and have our own views on love. But, I think the vast majority of us can agree on what love is NOT, and the things that PREVENT love from being made! We all could agree on the cliché things we wouldn't want our mate to do. Nobody wants a mate who is a liar, cheats, and things of that nature. Love is not built when those things keep occurring in a relationship. It's just easy to develop a tolerance for those things when you desperately want that person to love you. So many women have put up with men who take them through the lying and the cheating, and have fooled themselves into thinking they are in love. "Dope dick" or money is what normally has caused woman to stay in those types of relationships. And yes, "dope dick" is real. There are plenty of men who know as long as they keep bringing it in the bedroom then he will be able to stick around a lot longer. And, we all know what money will do to most people, so no need to get into that.

3) THERE IS ONE VERY IMPORTANT THING THAT I KNOW LOVE IS NOT, AND THAT IS IMPATIENT. I'm really aiming this towards women who have sex with a man to soon. "Well I know love can't be built overnight" or something of that nature is what some of you may be saying right now. But, why are so many GROWN women still using sex to keep a man around? So many women are well aware of the fact that if you don't give it up, he's not going to come around. But, you still do it hoping one day he will change. As complicated as love is, there is no way it can be built in a matter of days, a couple weeks, or a couple months. Sex is not a building block for love. Some women grow so impatient, that they SACRAFICE THEIR RIGHT TO HAVE A GOOD MAN. For the women who may say "all I wanted was sex anyway" need to refer back to definition of a double standard again. Read it one hundred times, please. And, the double standard will probably wreak havoc on your social life one day, as it does for so many women who just want sex. The impatient thing about love is simply due to one word. And that word is TEMPTATION.

It's difficult to concentrate with all of these temptations pulling at your arm, right?

A TEMPTATION IS AN ACT THAT LOOKS APPEALING TO AN INDIVIDUAL. IT IS USUALLY USED TO DESCRIBE ACTS WITH NEGATIVE CONNOTATIONS, AND AS SUCH, TENDS TO LEAD A PERSON TO REGRET SUCH ACTIONS FOR VARIOUS REASONS. TEMPTAION IS ALSO USED IN A LOOSE SENSE TO DESCRIBE ACTIONS THAT INDICATES A LACK OF SELF CONTROL.

Once again, these are not my words, but those in the dictionary. So, ask yourself this please. Have you ever been tempted to do the RIGHT thing? No, you haven't. You may have been reluctant or hesitant to do the right thing, but not tempted. We are tempted by things we know we SHOULDN'T do. The word TEMPTATION actually is deeply rooted in The Old Testament starting with the story of Adam and Eve. And, we all know what was unleashed due to a person who has circum to temptation in that story! Men certainly fall victim to temptations also, but we normally end up hurting women when we do. Men don't have the same repercussions of giving into temptations as a woman does, due to the double standard once again. So many people say that they are ready for LOVE, but they will settle for SEX. You HAVE sex, but you MAKE love. Do you know the difference? If you don't know the difference, and nobody is trying to show you, then you are just someone to HAVE, and nobody is trying to MAKE it in life with you. Stop having sex and start making love. Love is a thing that has to be built and is a mental battle that has unlimited rewards. Sex is simply a physical thing that any two fools can have.

4) PAIN IS NOT SOMETHING YOU GO THROUGH TO HAVE A SUCCESSFUL RELATIONSHIP, PAIN IS WHAT YOU GO THROUGH WHEN YOU ARE IN THE WRONG ONE. LOVE DOES NOT HURT. WHAT PAIN SHOULD SERVE AS IS A GREAT TEACHER. YOU ARE RESPONSIBLE FOR YOUR OWN HAPPINESS. IF YOU ARE DEALING WITH A PERSON WHO IS CAUSING YOU PAIN, THEN YOU ARE INSANE. TO KEEP DOING SOMETHING OVER AND OVER THAT YIELDS THE SAME RESULTS IS BASICALLY THE DEFINITON OF INSANITY.

Love is hard, but it does not hurt. There are women who actually think they have to wait until their trash becomes a treasure. Lot of Betty Wrights out here. A piece of man is not better than no man at all. She screwed the women with that one. Every relationship is a risk. Every relationship has its hardships. But, hard work ALWAYS pays off. You get rewarded for your hard work in a relationship, NOT PUNISHED. There are men and women who find every imaginary EXCUSE to stay in a bad relationship, and ignore the real REASONS they have to walk away. Love does not mean ignore reality. THERE ARE ONLY TWO REASONS A PERSON WON'T LOVE YOU THE WAY YOU DESERVE TO BE. 1) THEY DON'T KNOW HOW TO/NOT READY TO, so they can't, and you CAN'T be mad at them for that. 2) THEY DON'T WANT TO. Either way, you have to accept that. If you can think of any other reasons that make LOGICAL sense, please contact me! I'm willing to bet any other answer you can come up with is an EXCUSE, and not a REASON! Being in love does not hurt, losing love does. Accepting the truth about it is the one true way to relieve the pain. If you can't do that, then life will go on without you. You have to live in order to love again. You shouldn't have to wonder if your mate loves you or not. There are two things you can't hide from someone who is in love with you no matter how well you try to hide them. Those two things are happiness and unhappiness. Love is see-through. If the person you are in a relationship with can't recognize your constant signs of distress, then they are not in love with you. If they recognize it and don't care, then guess what?

When a woman knows and acknowledges her past, and is PROUD of it; ready to hold a man responsible for his actions, and believes what he DOES not says and doesn't just fall in love with the man himself; is patient enough to wait on a man to compliment everything she has going on; and realizes that love is not pain; I think she is on the right track and ready to accept a good man. Just know that EVERY relationship is a risk and a gamble. We often bet with our hearts, and that's OK. But, NEVER put your mind up to be lost. Don't let a person drive you insane. Put your own well being first. Just make sure your heart and your mind are not having an argument.

GMC

CHAPTER 6:

THE SINGLE LIFE BLUES

Being single is a time period of fun and freedom, right? This is a time in life when you don't have any obligations to anyone other than yourself. You are supposed to be free to do as you please. Well, that's basically true for children because relationships shouldn't be on their mind anyway. As an adult, the single life is the most important part of any future relationship you may have. This should be a period of PREPRERATION. Yes, you are free to go and do as you please under your own circumstances. Unless you are a parent you really don't have to take into consideration the feelings and well being of anyone but your own. But, if you have been having relationship problems in the past, or just haven't found "the one", then you can easily lose yourself or find yourself while you are single. I myself have experienced both and I'm sure a lot of you all have also.

What do I mean by "losing yourself" while you're single? This simply means worrying and stressing about being single. Being single is a great chance to consider any insecurities or mental barriers that you may have. Can you recall a point in your life when you just never thought you would find the right one? And, you finally found someone that you like but it just didn't work out at all. Or, it was maybe a disaster and you can't figure out what went wrong and how you even got into that situation? That may be what some of you are going through at this very moment. I want you to think back to the time before that relationship began. What were you doing while you were single? Can you honestly say your mind was at ease and being in a relationship was the least of your worries? If you can't, then the disaster started while you were single and not when you met that person. When you are stressing and worrying about finding someone, you don't make the best decisions. What happens is you meet someone you like and you go with that because the thought of being single again does not excite you. Now, the previous statement is true for people who are serious about having a successful relationship. Those of you that are living your life based on sexual needs are not interested in having a relationship, of course. Sex excites you. Sex excites me. Sex excites the majority of us. But, there will come a time when you are longing for more. And, you will have to put in the work it takes to become relationship material. The bulk of that work will and must be done while you are single.

So, what is the "work"? What can I do other than wait for the right person to come along? Well, you shouldn't be waiting for someone to come along. You're waiting on yourself. You're working on yourself. The most important thing to accomplish while being single is total honesty. You know what you want and how you want it. WOMEN tend to make more bad decisions than men while they're single. I say that simply because men can't get pregnant and men are not held to the same standards as women when it comes to sex. Again, RESPECT the double standard. It will protect a woman's social life. Am I somewhat making some sexist statements? No, because it's the truth. I'm not saying that men are free to do as we please while single. What I'm saying is that women have a lot more at stake than men. Men don't get pregnant and a man's reputation is not under the scrutiny that a woman's is. So, while a woman is single she can't afford to be as "open" as a man can. Is this a good thing for men? CERTAINLY it is not! Ladies, you make a man honor and respect his single life by simply honoring and respecting yours. Don't reward a man with the work you put in during your single life who obviously didn't put any into his. Two single people who were serious about their single life will add up to a serious relationship. A lot of us call that compatibility. That's how two people who didn't seem to have much in common found themselves to be a perfect match. They both were simply prepared for something real.

One sure way I know to prepare yourself for a relationship is to basically act like you're in one. Actually, you are in one. You are getting to know someone a little better every day, and it is you! I do think it's very possible to learn something daily. So, why can't that something you learn come from within on occasion? The things that make a relationship work may vary from couple to couple. But, we all know the things that will destroy a relationship. If you are single and the answer is yes to these following questions: you have more than one sex partner or "friend"; you enjoy clubbing and partying more than your own home (let's face the fact that clubs are hunting grounds for sex); you think the two previous questions I asked are irrelevant; Then you have just found out three reasons as to why your ass is single and can't make a relationship work. If you can't cut it in practice then you won't be ready for the real thing. Find something better to do with your time while being single. I'm definitely not saying that being a homebody is the way to be. I'm simply trying to differentiate between the mindset of a person who is preparing for a successful relationship, and one who is not.

And, to the playerettes out there. The women who constantly attempt to put themselves in a man's position. Let me put this to you delicately. You gotta have a dick to walk the walk we walk. And, you gotta have nuts to say the things we say. Why don't you strive to perfect the ways of a woman instead? I promise you that you'll receive all the things a woman deserves from a man in due time. As long as you are a woman who thinks she can get away with the same things that a man can, you'll never be the woman you need to be.

Fellas, I know that whenever we have had our feelings crushed by a woman the first thought sometimes is to find another one. Well, that's just the quick fix and you hinder yourself from growing as a man. If you're having woman problems, how can you solve woman problems with another woman? The rebound myth holds true for men and women. Again, take advantage of your single life and get yourself together. Being single and possibly going without sex for an extended amount of time is

MUCH harder for men in the beginning. Sometimes, that's just what has to be done.

There are those who are single who don't hang out in clubs, who are great with money, and have little to no sex life. All you do is visit with friends occasionally and go to work. You have been patient and not stressing at all about finding someone. You are perfectly comfortable with yourself. So, how long is my life going to be this way you might ask? It doesn't matter how long it last. You should be able to take solace in the fact that you are happy with yourself and have minimum stress. Sure, there are lonely nights and some anxious days. But, being single honestly doesn't bother you one bit. I myself have come to realize that being single is just as much of an opportunity at happiness as a relationship is. It's much easier for a relationship to flow when two people are not willing to risk a happy single life for a unprepared, unsure, stressed out person they just met.

No matter if you are single or not, the one thing you cannot allow yourself to be is SEDUCED. Well, what's wrong with being seduced you might asked? I'm a man who likes for words to actually APPLY to my situation. Once again, I must refer to the dictionary to define the word seduce.

Seduce: to persuade to disobedience or disloyalty; to lead astray usually by persuasion or false promises; to carry out the physical seduction of: entice to sexual intercourse; to lead away from duty, accepted principles, or proper conduct.

So, if I'm in a relationship then the word seduce shouldn't apply to me. I wouldn't want it to apply to me. My woman doesn't have to seduce me into doing anything with her. OK, maybe during a little role play it is fun to watch my woman practice the art of seduction. But hey, my mind was made up before hand anyway. She's just giving me WHAT I WANT. If I'm single, then why on earth would I want to be seduced? If a person has persuaded you to have sex with them, have you been seduced or actually reduced? Where you reduced to a person who has no self control? Where you reduced to a person who can't think for him/her self? Yeah, reduced seems more applicable. To you single people, I'm simply saying put in the work to make sure you don't get seduced. So I ask are we really seduced, or is that person just giving us WHAT WE WANT? Anyone who claims they were seduced by someone is trying to place the blame anywhere but themselves. They just gave you what you really wanted. Accountability and responsibility is what we're seeking here.

GMC

CHAPTER 7:

RETIRING HAS ITS UPS AND DOWNS

When a professional athlete retires from their sport, there are things that are good, and things that are not so good left to deal with. There are injuries and memories that last a lifetime. Well, same thing goes for the people who chose to play the game. Not all players and playerettes come out of this game with a happy ending. Some lives have been left in turmoil. And, it is very evident today. We see women who have been left to raise families by themselves. We have men who don't know the first thing about being a real man. Some exit the game with STD's they have to live with for life. Children are left to learn about life on their own. The majority of people who finally decide they want to be a respectful human being have to now learn how to become one. The questions I get asked are mostly by men and women who are at this point in life. They want a good relationship. They are tired of playing games. And, the women have grown impatient with men and want to really know what's going on. So, when a woman is MONOGOMOUSLY DATING and serious about finding, or has found a man, there are still things that raise serious questions. In this chapter I will basically discuss the questions I get asked the most, and I'm going to give it to you all RAW!

WHY DO MEN CHEAT? Of course this is the most frequently asked question by women. And CAN A MAN CHEAT ON A WOMAN THAT HE LOVES? Before I get into why a man cheats, let me tell women something about men and how we view women. You must understand how much of an influence you all have on a man's day to day decision making. Although men don't act like it at all times, besides life itself, men know that a WOMAN IS GOD'S GREATEST GIFT KNOWN TO MAN. Please understand that it is a daily struggle, even for the most honorable man, to deny himself these gifts. Especially when so many women are willing to give this gift to him for such small price. And, just to be blunt, men lie because a lie has become a small price to pay for some pussy. Men will try to avoid getting caught in a lie, but a man really doesn't care when he does. We care when you stop sleeping with us. Ladies, raise the stakes back up please. Demand his honor, his loyalty, his trust, and his commitment at ALL times. DEMAND IT AT ALL TIMES PLEASE.

There is no one particular answer to why a man cheats, but you may have heard the common answers. You may have heard that a man cheats simply because he can. Or, a man cheats because his woman allows him to do so. You may have heard that some men cheat because they are simply addicted to sex. All of these answers are true. But, those answers are just not good enough for some women. Well, don't expect to hear anything different from me. What I would hope a woman does is hold herself responsible for staying with a man who has cheated on her before. Once a cheater always a cheater? No, I wouldn't say that. But, in the SAME relationship where cheating has occurred that is a fact. Once a cheater always a cheater.

Can a man cheat on a woman he loves? No, he cannot. He can cheat on a woman he has love for. That means there are some things that he loves ABOUT her, therefore he is with her. I'm not willing to dishonor the word love and its true meaning by saying it can be dropped and picked up at anytime. Love does not cheat. And, you can't cheat love.

IF I CONSIDER MYSELF OUT OF THE GAME, WHAT AM I DOING TO ATTRACT PEOPLE WHO STILL WANNA PLAY? WHY DO I KEEP HOOKING UP WITH THE CHEATERS, LIARS, USERS AND ABUSERS?

First thing I want to discuss is a woman's attire. This subject gets to be the center of a discussion a lot. If you are a woman who wears a lot of revealing clothing, then what a man thinks of you initially will be revealed when he approaches you. Of course, there is a way to be classy as well as sexy, but some women go for the sexy, and forget the classy. Don't wear the whore uniform and expect not to get approached with little to no respect. I'm not justifying the disrespect a man can show, but don't let it surprise you is all I'm saying. As far as actually hooking up or seeing someone who turns out to be a loser, that's just the trials and tribulations of engaging in relationships. Every one of them will be a risk. This is all more the reason why women should not be so quick to sleep with a man. Just wait, be patient, and in due time everything you need to know will be brought to the light! Don't be mad because you encountered a man and he turned out to be a bad one. Only be mad if you stay with him. Also, you may keep attracting people who are not serious about having a relationship because you're not ready yourself. This goes back the single life chapter of the book. Are you sure you're prepared? End of story.

HOW LONG SHOULD I MAKE A MAN WAIT UNTIL WE HAVE SEX? AND, HOW LONG IS TOO LONG? I WANT TO MAKE SURE I'M READY BUT I DON'T WANT TO LOSE HIM.

As I stated earlier, I don't believe in putting a certain amount of time on having sex in a relationship. First, make sure that BOTH of you know that you are in a relationship! Not a friendship, but a relationship. If you are in a "friendship" then I guess it doesn't matter how long you wait. You're not supposed to be having sex anyway, so do as you please. Accountability and responsibility is what you need to be ready to fully accept. For those of you who are actually trying to develop a real relationship, just make sure that both of you are comfortable. Don't be afraid to discuss it with your man, ladies. If sex is what you want, then who am I to tell you to wait? If love is what you need and desire, then take the time to build it. You don't have to wait for sex, you wait for love. So take your pick. When a man is in it for the long run, he will wait however long it takes. Your comfort level is your comfort level, not his. Don't be mad about losing a man who was not willing to wait until you were ready to take that next step. If you are serious about having a relationship, then the emotional and mental support needed should outweigh the physical wants. So, until you are sure your mate can provide those things, sex shouldn't even be on the table. I just find it hard to believe that those qualities can be confirmed in a matter of hours, weeks, or a couple months. But, you be the judge! End of story.

WHY ARE MEN INTIMIDATED BY INDEPENDENT WOMEN, ESPECIALLY BY ONE WHO MAY BE MORE SUCCESSFUL THAN HIM? Men are not intimidated by a successful woman. Men simply have a need to feel needed and appreciated by their woman. Men are providers by nature. So, if the woman can provide for the relationship better than he can financially, then that's an adjustment not easily made. But, that's not an intimidation. If the woman is the bread winner in the relationship, she just needs to make sure her man is still able to play his role as a man. And, if you can't figure out how to do that, listen to the song "Cater to you" by Destiny's Child. Do whatever they said. End of story.

There are some women out here that are just too independent and feel they don't need a man for anything but sex. These women don't intimidate men, they repel them. A man who is serious about being a man doesn't want the woman that can do without him. End of story

A question that usually spawns from this same topic is HOW DO I LET A MAN BE A MAN. I know a man's pride can be his downfall sometimes. The one thing I want women to understand is that A MAN BEING OR BECOMING A MAN HAS NOTHING TO DO WITH A WOMAN. That is something he has to do on his own. HOW DOES A WOMAN HELP HER MAN WITHOUT ACTUALLY HELPING HIM?

A WOMAN HELPS HER MAN BE A MAN BY SIMPLY KEEPING HER STANDARDS AND NEEDS AT THE FOREFRONT. When a woman sticks to her guns and is demanding of her man, either he will step up to the plate and produce, or he won't. Demand that your man be a man at all times. This doesn't mean be critical, but just be sure he knows what you expect of him. There are some basic things a woman should not have to mention to her man. RESPECT is the main thing. If you find yourself constantly mentioning to your man that you don't feel respected, then you have a problem. And, if you are the reason your man has a car, new clothes, money in his pocket, basically his main support system then you have major problems. His woman should be a reason to push forward not the main reason he SEEMS to be moving forward. There are things that your man should have accomplished with you, not because of you. End of story.

SHOULD A WOMAN BE CHASING A MAN? Anything being chased doesn't want to be caught. A woman chasing a man? Really? Picture a cat chasing a dog. Can you see it? Does that look or even sound right to you? Enough said. And ladies, allow yourself to be PURSUED, not chased. A pursuit consists of well thought out steps. I'm pursuing a career in medicine sounds a lot more serious than I'm chasing a career in medicine, right? It's more than OK for a woman to express her interest in a man. After she has done so, she needs to allow the man to pursue her. Sort of like some animals do during mating season. Just show your pretty colors and wait for a man to approach you. If you don't approve, move on. End of story.

The most devastating thing that the game is responsible for are the broken homes we have today. The lack of irresponsibility and accountability is most evident when discussing why we have so many single mothers, and unreliable men. I get flooded with questions about the "baby daddy" or the "baby mama". The most FRUSTRATING thing to women is why the father of their child won't act the way they think he should. First let me say this, a "baby daddy" has been involved with a "baby mama". Think about that please. Make sure that you, the mother, are doing your part to make these situations as civil as possible. If you are the woman I see "showing her ass" in public then you are not helping the situation at all. We need more mothers and fathers. There are a couple of frequently asked questions about this subject that I wanted to go into.

There is one simple question asked a lot that has no simple answer, and that is WHY DOESN'T MY KID (S) FATHER WANT TO BE IN THEIR LIVES. Or, just why isn't he involved more? Let me explain the subtitle of my book, and I think it will give women and men a good understanding about this. I delayed explaining the subtitle of my book for questions like this.

A WOMAN'S UNCONDITIONED INTUTION, what good is it to her if conditioned under false pretenses? If women are getting their skills on dealing with the opposite sex sharpened by things they THINK men want and desire, how is that helping them? Although the "unconditioned intuition" label can primarily be aimed at the younger generation (18-30), that doesn't exclude the slightly older women. Yes, even some of you cougars out there have been engaging in relationships with no clue on what men like, or what men want. And if that's not true, then somebody please explain to me a forty year old, unmarried, slut. Don't act like there are not PLENTY of those walking around. There are women who have been living their entire lives trying to use what they got to get what they want, instead of using what they learned to get what they've already earned.

Child support was established in 1975. That was thirty-five years ago. Shout out to all the deadbeats of the 60's and 70's by the way. The men who are dealing with this system surely appreciate you. I mentioned the establishment of this system to prove a point. Men have been subpar for a while now, and that shouldn't be news to anyone. The fact that a system such as child support having to be launched is a testament to the fact that men have not been doing well for a long time. It became easier, cooler, more fun, and even more respectable to some people to play the GAME, as opposed to being a man who can respect women and raise a family. With the degrading of women on television, magazines, in music, and the other resources we have for entertainment, women have been fooled into thinking men will LOVE a particular type of woman. The sex selling, slutty clothing, down for whatever, gangster loving woman is who men have glorified, but they did so UNDER FALSE PRETENSES. Those are not the women who these guys actually look to marry and raise a family with. But, these are the women that men love to have sex with. Sadly, that is the prototype that a lot of women have chosen to aim for. Of course, there are women who didn't choose to be portrayed like this, but somehow found themselves in the same situations as the ones who did. Well, you may be a respectable woman who simply sacrificed her right to have a good man. Not all relationships work out, but all relationships have clear signs available to show you that they won't. We sometimes just choose to ignore them due to the fact that we simply are in love, or in strong like.

Something women need to understand is if you don't have a good man, then you won't have a good father to your children. That should really be a no brainer. Should a man take responsibility for any child he helps create? Absolutely he should. Is he going to be committed to raising a child when he wasn't committed to the relationship to begin with? There's a high possibility that he won't. Women who get pregnant in the game have violated the rules. Men who get women pregnant in the game have violated the rules. It's just unfortunate that women are the ones left to deal with the child alone in most cases. Like I said while explaining the game earlier, sex or money is the objective. Men don't feel responsible for the woman or the child. A lot of women are jumping into the game and getting pregnant, and want the game to STOP right then and there. Men are in the game getting women pregnant and don't give a damn about changing his lifestyle at all. This is simply irresponsibility on behalf of them both. "But, I was everything he wanted me to be". This is what a woman is thinking, and not being everything SHE wanted herself to be. Yes, you were everything he wanted you to be as long as you didn't get pregnant. "Unplanned pregnancies" are about as real as fried ice cream. So, as long as you are having sex, you have no choice but to expect to get pregnant. But, don't expect that man to feel the same way that you do about it. And, realize that you have no control over him being a good father or not. If you were involved in a relationship that just didn't work out, and the father is not up to par, there is not much you can do to change him. What more can I say, manhood is not given, it's earned. Some men have a hard time supporting something they are not a part of. Of course, some men don't want the kid(s) unless he can have the woman. There a various EXCUSES as to why men are not better fathers and men in general. But, I can tell you this. It is nearly impossible for a man to mistreat a good woman, because she is good to herself FIRST. A woman's intuition can be molded by the games we play for fun, or by the games she left behind. It's her choice. Sad to say.....but hurt feelings, emotions, and even kids get charged to the game sometimes. End of story. Do you still want to play?

Being that I didn't want to be religiously biased, I only made one reference to GOD in this book. I accepted Jesus Christ as my Lord and savior a long time ago, and I know that ALL things are possible through GOD. There are exceptional men throughout the world who follow and practice religions that differ from mine. But, as I mentioned in my description of what The GMC stands for, we all should have a common line of thinking when it comes to manhood, especially if you are a citizen or residing in the United States of America. My passion to see women doing well, and people in general is genuine. I was humbled a long time ago as well. This book was not for a financial gain, nor an attempt to raise my stock with the ladies. I have acquired and lost those things before throughout life. This book is simply a declaration of everything I believe in when it comes to women and manhood. The things I have been through and witnessed have been diagnosed and put on paper, then explained the best way I can in order to show women how important they are. Never sacrifice your right to have a good man. Any woman who doesn't know she is beautiful and priceless will end up with a man who tells her the same thing. You ALL are beautiful. You ALL are worthy. **End of story.**